THE RESURRECTIONISTS

John Challis was born in London in 1984. His pamphlet, *The Black Cab* (Poetry Salzburg, 2017), was a 2019 New Writing North Read Regional title. He has received a Pushcart Prize and a Northern Writers' Award. In 2015 he was a poet-in-residence with the Northern Poetry Library and chosen as one of the Poetry Trust's Aldeburgh Eight. His poems have been broadcast on BBC Radio 4, and published in journals including *Ambit*, *Magma*, *The North*, *Poetry Ireland Review*, *Poetry London*, *The Rialto* and *Stand*. John also writes reviews and essays, most recently for *Wild Court*, *PN Review*, *Poetry Salzburg Review* and The Poetry School.

He holds a PhD in Creative Writing from Newcastle University, where he currently works as a Research Associate. His first book-length collection, *The Resurrectionists*, was published by Bloodaxe in 2021. He lives in Whitley Bay.

JOHN CHALLIS

The Resurrectionists

BLOODAXE BOOKS

ISBN: 978 1 78037 551 9

First published 2021 by
Bloodaxe Books Ltd,
Eastburn,
South Park,
Hexham,
Northumberland NE46 1BS.

www.bloodaxebooks.com
For further information about Bloodaxe titles
please visit our website and join our mailing list
or write to the above address for a catalogue

Supported using public funding by
**ARTS COUNCIL
ENGLAND**

Cover design: Neil Astley & Pamela Robertson-Pearce.

Printed in Great Britain by Bell & Bain Limited, Glasgow, Scotland, on
acid-free paper sourced from mills with FSC chain of custody certification.

For Kris and Fern

CONTENTS

And if I can keep secrets for years,
The way a stone retains a warmth from the sun,
It is because men like us
Own nothing, really.

LARRY LEVIS

The Love

Where does it go? Depots mainly, on the edge
of Kent and Essex. Try the Dartford Crossing –
sewage plants, substations, heavy traffic –
a perfect place for murder. They keep it stocked
in wooden crates on endless shelves
floor after floor in subterranean bunkers:
love contained like unsold cargo
or un-pulped books; the self-help kind, flat-packed love
for easy storage, love damp and jaundiced.
Love worn on no one's sleeve, love rattling
like shattered ceramics on the tusks of a forklift.
How does it get here? It just comes
for early career researchers, who mill about the aisles
dressed in protective suits, who unearth
platonic love from cases, like plutonium,
careful not to spill a drop of all this used
and wasted love. They've heard the rumours,
spots, blindness, madness, mania, jealous rages,
fits and giggles, genocide. Winners
of the Turner Prize shipped in to build collages
chronicle its decline, or replicate Rodin's
The Kiss from never-worn engagement rings,
dredged from drains, rivers, pawn shops,
and lovelocks clipped from the Pont des Arts
to ease the weight of love. Musicians digitise
the sound, moans like warping steel or wood,
the chorus of an altered mass. Meanwhile,
the poets, wearing rubber gloves, read charred
and tea-stained letters, cached emails
from dumped lovers, to recycle Eros
from the mulch of this organic compost.

in my heart

there's a market full of men
who want attention to their bargains who
are yelling to the point of inflammation
of the bronchi of swooning blue-faced
into the haze of fruit-flies bothering
over-ripe tomatoes
years of lifting boxes
of their perishable livelihoods they suffer
groin hernias spinal strains slipped discs
but can't afford the time to mend –
the meat and veg are on-the-turn the stink
has lured the foxes
this they gripe to keep
their homes and live the so few hours
when the awnings of their hearts
relax their little pinches

To a Coal-fired Power Station

Daily, you wake up to fire up the furnace
    to burn and to steam for us, who believe
but hardly dare show it – praying in private
    as we blush into mirrors, drying our hair
with your breath from our sockets,
    speaking on phones, you listening in
and watching through eyes of the filaments.
    You are always there, the church no one visits.

They'd rather scorn your hard appearance.
    A brutal eyesore. A functional ruin.
Pamphlets are written and passed on the campus.
    Speeches given on high streets, in halls.
Some, camped on the slagheaps, protest.
    They want to see your cooling towers
fold inwards and crumble into sinkholes.
    When the picture's big enough, Parliament speaks.

In Yorkshire, I can see you for miles,
    you concrete pig, fattened on coal,
on your back kicking your stubby trotters.
    If you were suddenly granted life, would you rise
to level Northumberland wind farms,
    to trample the fields of solar panels
so fiercely the Earth would tremble, to bring
    nuclear meltdown across the meadows?

In a dream I had, we queued outside,
    and when you began to throw up the smoke
we came in to give our confessions
    by throwing ourselves onto the flames

as renewable biomass. I woke up sweating
   before you recast our flesh in the form
of yourself and installed on our mantelpieces
   shrines we could never ignore.

On clear days I've taken your portrait,
   your majestically rising staircase of steam,
and shared it online to a hundred *likes*.
   When you are gone, like the mines
we have flooded, when you are only a pile of rubble,
   we'll fondly remember the look that you gave,
colossally Roman; a wound in the earth
   scabbed-over and cut off to keep the country lit.

Your plume seeps like a net catching
   towns your shadow can never leave.
You haunt them like an oil spill.
   And once we have sacked and pillaged the temple,
stripped it of assets and sold off the plot,
   there'll be something of you left in the soil.
Plague ground we cannot forget; the price
   we paid for our world with the world's blood.

Plague Ground

I *2013*

At Farringdon Crossrail my spade struck
neither leather ball nor ceramic bowl,
but a seventeenth-century plague victim's skull.
Heavy. Its sockets were filled with muck.

As I held his skull I thought of the sod –
on fire inside, no anaesthetic.
I took a photo of bones arranged like sticks
in the plot where death laid him, where now I stood.

II *1665*

I stood in the plot where I laid him dead.
Dead from his groin to his arm-pit cave
where boils throbbed till he coughed up raves
of blood. A corpse cushioning his head.

Commissioned to dig the old graves free,
I dug the fragments of fibula and femur,
the bones of the fourteenth century,
until the soil was shovelled clean.

III *1348*

Back into digging, I shovelled the turf
over my shoulder until six feet deep
my spade struck rock. I pushed the heap
of gangrened bodies, smoothed over the earth.

Hammered a post, no monument
or list of stone-carved names, but a caution
Do Not Cross This Land, this hastily undone
field, plagued at Farringdon, north of London.

Advertising

All night they have been touching meat,
thrusting trolleys stuffed with cheek,
shoulder, ear and leg, and now the day's
come back to life they're closing
Smithfield market; sewing up the partly
butchered, washing off the blood.

I watch them from my office vantage
stripping their overalls. I button up
my collar for handshake after handshake,
presenting our creative for clients to dissect.

The past is lowered like a theatre set.
Axes swing for human heads, the gallows
start their jig, men sell unwanted wives,
and horseshit is piled high beside meat labelled fresh.

Preservation in Situ

We know these people weren't the poorest,
buried with their knives and buckles, beads and pins

to trade in the afterlife for entry
or a faster path through whichever

underworld or heaven they imagined.
So who else can it be, who gives this wind

such a solid punch? Who else but the ones
whose bones are not recorded?

Laid to rest in clay, no tributes
for the doorman, turned away from every gate

like paperless immigrants.
Of course they're angry, they aren't afraid to show it

by dialling up the Beaufort scale,
by moving the inanimate, by whisking

sand and sea spray into full-bodied clouds.
They too are here in situ at Bamburgh,

skulls and femurs ground to dust, feeding
the colonies of dune grass and mushroom.

As in their lives, they give themselves,
teeth bared to show us where they're from.

This is the market

the cauliflower business in this town is down the drain

BERTOLT BRECHT, *The Resistible Rise of Arturo Ui*

        Bundled first editions arrive.
Comics released from West End clubs
rehearse new material to labourers and foremen.

Authority figures stride to cars from young men
getting dressed in alleys. A bottle smashes.
A cab beeps. Laughter swells from opened café doors.

I used to treat the children on Fridays.
Fish wrapped up in the *Evening Standard*.
Or trips to Clacton on Saturday mornings.

Now I bring home things I am given.
Boxes of shirts stacked in the hallway.
Our cupboards stocked with premium tea.

It was found in the street abandoned.
It fell off the back of a lorry. Came our way
after the death of a long-lost Irish cousin.

Money is found in the strangest places:
the wheel-arch of a delivery van;
wrapped in a bag in a toilet cistern; under

a copper's Custodian Helmet. Ownership is fluid.

The Knowledge

Not the knowledge chosen for the national
syllabus, nor knowledge scrawled by Mrs Smith
on the board in shaky chalk, but the knowledge
I heard my father practise, out loud after tea.

Not a knowledge of capital cities, of England's
football captains, David Beckham's scoring record,
nor any pub quiz question, but a knowledge of maps,
of London's maps in more than three dimensions.

Maps that covered the dining room, a cheap print
of *The Hay Wain*, of *Bubbles* and our photographs.
Maps he rose each day to enter, a clipboard
on his handlebars, to expand his hippocampus.

Manor House to Gibson Square; Archway
to Gloucester Gate; Penn Street to Portland Place;
Consort Road to MoD
via Peckham Rye and Westminster Bridge.

But I can't buy the wisdom that vocation
is hereditary – that sons should give their lives
to do the jobs their fathers did – instead, I learnt
not from the front, but from the back seat of his cab

ferrying decision-makers, Canary Wharf
to Portcullis House, past navvies tunnelling
the Underground, through the husk of blackout
London, and to here and now: this argument.

Taught to speak by sixteen years of answering
the register, by milk, chalk and cartridge ink,
Shakespeare and the Lord's Prayer, I raise my arm
to pay my coins, my tributes to the knowledge.

Horses in Upton Park

I hadn't expected horses, splendid
in their yellow smocks and welders' visors.
What they must have thought of us.

They lived in stables or on scrapheaps
by motorways. Stunted ones, peppered white,
wearing ornately coloured saddles,

bore the weight of children at primary
school fêtes. Deep down a country lane
a sudden swift galloping blind to ambler

or canine comes. These were different.
Police horses. Sleek and obedient. Strangers
to fording polite streams under full moons,

they must dream of acting as statues to anger.
And why they still choose them over
armoured vehicles? The wildness of horses.

How their hooves can crush a man's temple
with a kick. How, when you're close enough
to look into a horse's eye,

a blacksmith is firing his forge. I'd reach
to stroke a mane but there is sudden news
of an engagement with away support,

and when what seemed born to stillness moves,
there's fear beyond language that sets itself
amongst your bones as though someone's

suddenly there in the back of your car,
at the foot of your bed, rearing like a horse
on its hind legs. And the terrible sound

of braying penetrates and freezes
and the dark and wild stare becomes the night
before the first of us found the gift of fire.

Hansard

I've been writing elegies for the undead.
Imagining the hovels where their souls will be sent,
and making sense of their still-in-use possessions.
I'm pressing ears to walls and doors, and taking
the minutes of the air, my pen on paper
a cardiograph. I'm planning funerals ahead.
But nightly, ghosts arrive with tickets to the picture house
to see a film from *their time*, shot in black and white,
with the pale leads dressed in 'old-style hats and coats'.

And even though we spoke this morning, I see
my teenage father help the Rt Hon. George Brown
rise out of the gutter, with Dave Darkins and a copper,
as I walk past Downing Street, no armed guards or cameras,
to a black cab on Whitehall. No waiting paparazzi.
My father's on a year of half-nights, printing
Hansard from the Commons. I hear him whisper
as I stroll: 'I signed the Official Secrets Act.'
Smug to know the price hike before the printers' local.

And as I write some copy on a client's APRs,
I hear myself say to him: 'Dad, you ever get creative?
Change the words? Revise the budget?'
'No, never, not our place. We left the lies to higher men.'
And as I get this down on paper, I watch him prime the typeset,
see him hold his inky hand, much younger than I am now,
to pass the baton, no, the torch, no, a cloudy pint.
Now here's my mother's father who never touched a drop,
lighting up to watch TV. I ask him what's on

but his eyes and mouth are stitched up and I do not have the heart.

The Last Good Market

Being faithless, I've always preferred to think of death
as the end of a movie, no sequels
or questions, the final scene as clear as glass,
no room for misinterpretation or for reading into
by sceptical scholars; this one's for the pragmatists
who like to know the end before it starts.

But watching Eileen on the day that we cremated Fred
had me thinking of a compromise, how after all there might be
somewhere they all congregate, worn out
from the journey across the barren afterlife.
Take your pick: the golden city,
the courtyard made of cloud, or the house

that you were born in. Though I can't shake
the feeling that nurses rouse to empty wards
with no one but themselves to heal, and from blackboards
teachers turn to classrooms of abandoned chairs and desks,
and that one day my father will wake up from snoring
in his black cab to wait for no fares on the rank.

But there are those of us who like our work,
and glad again to be of use, Fred is lifting up
the muddied sacks in the last good market,
admiring how his muscles flex, to fill the stall
with growth as fresh as the January morning
when he slipped out of his suffering and beyond

the fruitless task of dreaming up the ways
that faith employs the dead. I know that we must let them rest.

But I'm compelled to speak of what at night they show me:
the streets where they hold daily market,
where they shout their throats red-raw
and serve their last deductions on imperishable goods.

The District Line

If you ride the train to the end of the line,
keys in your fist for the robbery districts,

if you sit for an hour, your city in the window,
as roads laid over roads laid over dirt laid over bones

turn slowly into fields, where the only towers are chapels
standing firm over parishes of graveyards over

graveyards, then you'll have to peel away the masks
you've worn over the years, the selves

tried on for pleasure, to conform or please another,
that never grafted properly.

And even when you think you've found yourself
staring from the window, reflected over marshlands,

there's a tremor underneath your cheek,
that shows you what you've always known.

Inside Time

The quiet courtyard fills with rain that drives across
the floodlights. Along the cloisters, guards as dark
as seals in rubber coats are lumbering between
the gates with chains of silver keys. Rain drips

from barbed wire that coils at every concrete edge
where security finds seagulls, snagged up and torn apart
by their own attempts to leave. Beyond the twelve-
foot wall, new builds boast their Christmas lights.

The guards won't let their daughters go to parties
in these close-to-prison houses, afraid of breakouts,
where inmates unstitch themselves to throw
their bodies, limb by limb, over steel-mesh fences.

In these cabins where the view only ever changes
when it rains like this, or snows, a man may carry such an image
inside his head for years, and hang it above his pillow
to cool off in tar-scented summers. The ground becomes

a window. Outside, the news is waiting with a knife
behind its back. On the wing, the men in socks and sweats
heat up frozen pizzas and chalk their cues to strike
the best breaks of their stay. Rain soothes the windows

of this hyper-managed campus. And a man from Plaistow writes
'O lord, free the wood pigeon. She is my neighbour.'

Deadman's Walk

The last man to be hanged in public,
Michael Barrett undergoes a quiet word with Christ
and walks the narrow passage through
the bowels of Newgate Prison, his mind fixed
on the populace gathered in gin shops
where bookies calculate odds on whether
he'll survive the drop, while Jack Ketch
swings from Gimonde's fit-up, *that's the way
to do it!* as a galloping in his gut begins,
the scene already pencilled in for the *Illustrated
London News*, the instant when his neck
will stretch like a chicken's, his legs invite
a yanking from the crowd to end it faster,
and bartering for inches of the hanging rope

begins. No matter the crime,
rats arrive with sicknesses, and London's
lost rivers rise to flood the cells
with sewage. Lucky for the hapless Fenian
to have made it from the cruciform
buried under Clerkenwell, that shape
of Roman punishment we dangle
from our necks, where darkness siphons
fat reserves, sharpening every edge.
To earn a place by God they come
at soiled dawn to watch the workmen
build gallows and line roads
with barriers, a nervous cheer
escaping those who like to hear rope

tautening, the singing chord
of the noose. Right-hand man
of Christ behind him, Michael
Barrett almost buckles, ducking
through gradually narrowing
arches. Drowning in the curses
seen fit to coin by God, ahead
the doorways taper, diminishing
to focus him on this backwards
birth into the dark. He is so thin
he hardly needs to turn his waist
to fit through the concertina
of upright coffins that size
him down to fit the waiting

hole. If cruelty
were an architect
this passage
is its masterpiece.
Michael Barrett
steps to meet
the noose's
open mouth
that wants
to weed out
Michael
Barrett's spine
with a short
sharp

snap.
Then voices
calling through
the silence:

fresh fruit
and
cockles
and
eel pie
and
mussels
and
oysters
alive

Thames

After a day of keeping tugs and waste disposal barges,
sailing racers, showboats and commuter clippers afloat,
the Thames turns inwardly to find a space
to stretch out in, within a space no bigger than itself,
and burrows through the mud and clay
where every London intersects, to get its nose beneath the grave,
then flips the past up like a coin to send afloat
its drowned possessions: Anglo-Saxon ornaments,
unexploded payloads, bone dice and oyster shells,
wedding rings and number plates, and all those
you might have been had your time started early:
grave-diggers, barrow boys, mole men and cockle pickers,
gong farmers and costermongers, resurrectionists
and suicides; the taken, the lost, the given –
then settles down to dream again of all its infant waterways,
the estuaries and tributaries that led it here,
among the rusted hulls of years, to where there is no space
to breathe or settle down to sleep.

The Origin of Coal

The heart waited for its body on a beach.
Each dog tried to claim it by urinating

on the heart. The gulls were equally infatuated
but the heart was far too heavy

for any gull to carry. Alone, the heart reminisced
to feel it purr inside the body.

It thought about the chest-beating fights
that left its body breathless.

Each wave breaking brought the pounding closer.
Night brought other challenges.

Below where the heart rested, just above
the waterline, small eruptions moved the heart

closer to the water. On those nights of migration
the moon would cool and freeze the heart,

barely a tremor inside itself to know it was alive.
By this time the heart had blackened,

so much so no one noticed the heart
was still a heart. Women threw it for their dogs.

And the gulls didn't bother working the tough
jerky of its skin. It waited and it waited

for somebody to recognise the heart for who it was,
and dreamed of being put back

into the chest from where it fell, beating
its burning chambers as though it could fly.

There may be thawing damage

(after Robert Ettinger and Jo Shapcott)

Our inclination is to make do with imperfection.
This practice is derived from an article entitled

Several Types of Death. The rich alone are able
to invest in the absurd and the impractical.

But we must be in no doubt of our direction.
Let us review the findings. Upon a patient's death,

which we define as 'clinical', perforate the body
to assimilate the material. Enclose it in an envelope

of copper, bronze, nickel, nitrogen or gold.
Dr Parkes defines the second type as 'biological'.

If it is beyond us to resuscitate a subject,
he encourages experiment. This seems only logical:

our progress does not depend on any special
timetable. If practised accurately, the patient's blood

is substituted. The third and final type we fear
is sadly irreversible. We must work fast to prevent

degeneration of the body's cells. Such tragic
alterations temper a subject's character. Or soul.

Although it is impossible to suspend the narrative,
deterioration is arrested by storing the body at

a very low temperature. We grant ourselves
the chance to taste the wine of centuries unborn.

Gift of the Gab

Closing time. Market traders wrap
their gifted tongues in greaseproof paper.
They transplant vivid steaks

to cold drawers and the walk-in fridge,
from where my granddad steps
with a chilled-blue face.

His language is foreign.
I can't translate the weights and measures
on this avenue of butchers' shops.

It should be in my blood,
his knack for selling, his spiel and patter,
but I'm more at ease with the cleanliness

of what the market has become.
An emporium of artisan: bistros,
vintage clothes and specialist obsessions,

cupcakes and paella dishes – silent
and arranged where the dead still slash
sacks of sawdust open. They hang

rabbits like wrung-out rags,
singing with their strong tongues of kilogram
and stone, of shilling, pence and pound.

In Praise of the Flood

Gulls sharpen their beaks on the tarmac.
The clothes on the line are parched.
There are no dogs.
They are banned for the season
which might become unending.

I immerse myself under the cold,
let water do what it's meant to do.
The foghorn blows
and I cease to be an island.
The tankers have nowhere to dock.

In the city, water alights
from the metro, or so the headlines
would have us believe.
No one is where they need to be.

Things can only get better

Mine is the first generation able to contemplate the possibility
that we may live our entire lives without going to war or sending
our children to war.

TONY BLAIR, Paris, May 1997

The war was shot and screened at night.
Eddie arrived with barely a word of English.
At the old doctor's a flag was hanging
with a red star in the middle. We filled
our socks with water and we threw them
like grenades. We tied our soldiers to sticks,
surrounded them with toilet paper,
lit the pyre and watched their faces melt.

At the school fête a recruitment officer
showcased a Browning. We rolled pears
beneath oncoming traffic. The unloaded bazooka
weighed as much as a cardboard tube.
We had to peel the flattened pears
from the tarmac with our fingernails.
I knocked for Eddie one afternoon.
There was a white shape where the flag

had hung. The living room was empty.
We pretended we were medics. We lifted up
the spattered fruit onto the stretchers
of our hands. Of Tony Blair I first recall
the advertising and the song. I climbed
into the cockpit of the Challenger
and made explosion sounds. We left
the yield of split pears rotting in the bucket.

Entrenched

I couldn't see where the sound was coming from.
But I heard Big Ben chime the pub to silence.
Everyone was a monument. I thought about the losers.

What of *their* ended love affairs? *their* mother's little soldiers
sent off with their bellies full? *their* fatherless daughters?
My grandfather said remembrance was self-righteous;

there was nothing worth remembering. He sold his medals
on the doorstep to a man who preyed upon the old
for widows' bargain gold. They offered all kinds down the market –

boxes full of wedding rings
that never found inheritors, or if they did were pawned
to pay the bills, the bailiffs and the boatman.

Stars for France and Germany, for Burma and the Arctic,
Territorial, Mercantile and Victory decorations,
Stahlhelms and Lugers and Swastika armbands.

In Romford somewhere a lockup's stocked with retired booty
wanting to be robbed, wanting to be posted back
to pensioners like postcards from their younger selves,

like little pleading elegies. I heard the bugle's charm,
the sanitised announcer. And on the other side of silence
cold yolks were opened up, bacon worked on with a knife.

The room was full of voices. And the bar ten deep.

B Road Lay-by

Wind down the window: onions fry in lard,
an inch-thick beef patty whispers on a grill.
Other seasons offer a stall of Kent cherries,
blackberry and Braeburn juice or doughnut peaches.
But tonight the menu's meat: cow, pig, maybe horse
for lorry drivers, RAC vans, the family on a shoestring,
the learner restricted to non-lit passages,
the country's near forgotten maze of beta roads.

OK Diner, the Little Chef, Little India, Chinese China,
the UK's *largest* adult store, all closed for the night.
The Roman keep, the botanic garden, the steam
railway museum, the battle site, the ruined fort,
the *secret* Cold War mausoleum have sent
school tours and eager parents away to view the present.
Ketchup-covered tabloids pile up in bins,
their dates mashed together by cold tea and rain.

This plot, partitioned from empire, is a slip road
out of England. There's no MP or constituency.
There's no one to blame. A tree full of Tesco bags
rattles like a broken toy. A rusted Ford Granada rests,
clapped-out and burnt. Clamped by an oak's trunk
it is a playground of vines with an 80s mixtape
unspooled in the glovebox. Relief, sought in ragged
scrub, abuts *Auto Trader* and a spoon.

With the company of his generator rattling close
to expiration, he'll fuel those who chance upon this back-
neck of nothing where carbonised St George flags
are lifeless in the wind. Twice, the van with *CLEAN ME*

fingered on its rear, pleads to remain ungoverned
in this scrubland of a hamlet. But on the third,
against the odds, the van gasps into life and reignites
the night; there are miles still on the clock.

Where the devil gets in

All present and correct: the parcels of mown ground,
ruled lines of hedges, rectangles of ploughed mud,
scraggy fringes of silver birches dangling over fences,
their buds right-angled to accommodate the lorries.

But a sense of our bare selves lurks in the soil
and rises when it rains, the ground as bloated as a man
pulled from the river. Drains empty the understreet
and run along the kerb: new streams to be named

should they stay the course and widen over driveways
and welcome mats, and the country become a filter
for poor taste and bad vibes drawn from the groundwater,
stagnating on the green and pleasant lawns.

All graves flung open

Most films have them half-together,
walking through forest parts at the edge of town.

Perhaps they're moaning, uncomfortable
in rotten shoes, toothless jaws too slack for words.

They have no memory. This town they knew,
its bowling greens and takeaways and discount shops

where they cursed for hours the hikes
in council tax, a meatless nowhere to them now.

They shamble like blackout drunks, drawn
by muscle memory to cul-de-sacs, fumbling for keys

beneath doormats and flowerpots,
as a motion sensor light snaps and shocks them

to their former selves, long enough to see
in blacked-out windows the villains they've become.

Ballad Night at Sgt Peppers

Another bar: the orange kept-in light gone bad,
its two-for-ones and silver taps,
a siren song to thirst. I find my seat,

acknowledging my fellow mourners,
each attending their private wake:
the corner booth, the casket

of the self they were an hour ago,
a line of empty glasses.
Tonight, I'll visit each of you,

to hear how well or badly everything is going,
while someone sings a song that nobody
should ever hear too often.

Sold at the roadside in hell

In hell the roadside flowers flower
brilliant reds. The red of irritated eyes,
inflamed and rash-red skin. I buy
a bunch of red-flowered mallow.
Get in my red and burning car
(another scorching day in hell)
and drive to your apartment. I listen
to the radio, to hell's premier
FM station: *Great Balls of Fire*,
Disco Inferno, come on baby *Light
My Fire*, hell, it's gettin' *Hot
in Herre*; hits by famous residents.
I am a nobody. Another lost lover,
somewhere in the backcountry,
circling the city with my burning gift.

Resurrectionists

I

Some nights I leave out
milk and bread. They arrive in silence,
no fanfare of ice on breath,

and take their place
as though they've always sat there,
weighing their words.

They speak in turn:
the rivers I failed to dredge,
the fields of wheat hissing around a knife.

I follow the crumbs they scatter
on their way back to their deathbeds.
I see if one will let me crawl into their grave.

II

You know the men whose business
is to bring the dead to surgeons
so that they may live again,

jerking on the table
at the dawn of electricity,
convulsing for the benefit of students?

I too feel the urge to make something
out of nothing and profit from this work:
the page my barrow and my charge the word.

III

I hold the tally meter and count the dead
as they arrive, thrown in
through the doorway

of the ground. I interview and catalogue,
I note and name the battlefield: preserving
with my rituals of bog, clay and peat, I build

a bibliography of bone.
To comprehend the narrative
I taste the dirt that lingers in their mouths.

IV

Because I do not plant or seed you will not call me
gardener. And yet I work to aid the spring.
I give my days to cultivate the earth with lower homes.

Though who would argue what I do applies
a draughtsman's artistry, but those like me who dig
the holes, who prep and lay the bulbs?

When someday I own a plot of all I gave my life to know,
with every shoot and bud you find, remember
this is me, still labouring below.

Into the Maze

This summer of our Uni friends getting hitched
in country houses, endless in its bookings
of service station Travelodges, I plead with you:
relent, give me my weekends back.
I cannot bear to wear the grey (it oppresses
like a wetsuit) or noose the skinny tie I'm told
that fashion now dictates, or swab my brogues
for spots of sick from Halifax last week.

Spare me the hours starving while the couple
act contented near the giant chess board,
the ivy-strangled archway, the hired,
polished, horse-drawn carriage that almost
turned the nervous stomachs of the newlyweds.
Instead I choose to follow her into the stately
labyrinth, its walls of English Yew
grown tall as though to mute the flashbulbs.

In the centre is no golden falcon, no man-
beast minotaur, nor the spandex-wearing
David Bowie juggling crystal balls
(the opening of *Let's Dance* on the ear's mind
from the distant PA), but the wilderness,
un-manicured, no walkways and no mile-posts,
no half-worn desire paths. Canapés offered DIY.
The best man's speech diminishes.

Godless in these heavens without a camera
bent on conservation, memory is put to time's
unaided test of sense. No flute to drink from,
fork to spear with, only hands to hunt and pick,

to jimmy roots, to gather firewood
and divine the spark to warm her skin,
here in our cabin built of air alone,
I'll study under her to learn all nature's names.

The moth collector

One could not help watching him
VIRGINIA WOOLF

The moth collector spends his Friday nights
identifying moths. It frustrates him when Virginia

Woolf doesn't name the moth. Only a few
species are attracted to the light. It isn't moths

themselves that eat our rugs and woollens
but the larvae laid by certain kinds

of moths. Some of them are Angle Shade,
Cinnabar, Scalloped Oak, and need to be dissected

to be named. In the moth collector's
world at night he doesn't change into a moth.

The moth collector in his shed, a single lamp
burning, categorises moths by the aid

of *The Field Guide to Moths of Great Britain*.
He subtracts moth from moth

until he has removed the bead of life.
He pins their wings, lays them out, nothing left

behind, beneath or within to learn about
the moth. The moth collector goes to sleep.

And while the moth collector sleeps, he breathes
into the room an eclipse of Hoary Bells

and Chimney Sweepers, Poplar, Lime and Privet
Hawks. Though only in his dreams does

the moth collector witness how the nameless
circle a dangling moon.

Naming the Light

We've christened light as *light* but it has no
knowledge of the name. It doesn't notice how
it falls between the branches and the blinds,
or how it casts a glow on us, who rise
to meet its wakening in every living form.
Don't cheapen it as the reward, it doesn't think
itself the doing of the Lord. It has no mind
to show the way when everything has burned.

When we face the darkness, *light* will fall
out of our language. I know if I'm to name this,
this lost-for-words I feel with you
that I would call the Lord's work if I were
a man of faith, the word would never do.
And would I want to, when our silence is enough?

How to disable the alarm on a Saab 9000

> And whereas writing can comment upon its own limits, images must
> remain silent regarding their own perfections and imperfections.
>
> SUSAN STEWART

Staying still's not in his nature so this cannot be accurate
and will remain unfinished. But I've started, so let me try
even though he's gone already, is driving on the highway
pursuing sun and half-way now to Baker in his ever-filthy Saab,

but as usual he's left the door unlocked, so let's go in
and look around at what he's left behind – the way he cannot
rest beneath a ceiling, how he keeps internal spaces
moving as though a wind is blowing, his apple cores

and dental floss and ear plugs and running shoes
constantly in action. Though, like I said, he's gone,
is half-way up the mountain, offering his anecdotes
on love life or climate change to anyone on switchbacks.

And I haven't even started on the outline of his skull,
so I'll have to try another way which cannot do him justice,
because all I've heard since I arrived is how
when things aren't going well his temper is a forest fire.

Naturally, you understand, I have to mind my words
lest I end up like the others who could never please her father.
So let me end by focussing on the golden light that casts
his aura onto aerials and chimney tops,

wherever I see it falling, the light that sets the peaks ablaze
that right now he must be summiting, at his only tidy spot
on Earth, and staking out his Double Rainbow
before the summer drought begins, before the fires start.

North Cascades

I *Running at Altitude*

Up this high and working hard,
the capillaries in our lungs
have fattened like a bunch of grapes.
We're spitting nickels
on Hart's Pass, a one-lane
gravel road of unguarded vertigo
to the fire lookout,
as if some violence wanted out of us.

We saw a clear cut earlier.
The smell of fresh felling
sweet and narcotic.
They dragged the pine
from the shape of itself
and pulled it like a puppet
that was suddenly aware
and trying to shake off the master's hand.

II *On Sourdough*

As the sun slinks behind
Mounts Fury, Terror, Challenger,
headlights move like satellites
orbiting the mountain roads.

We've drunk our hot chocolate
and said goodnight to all of this:
the pain of hiking switchbacks
over six thousand feet,

to the bears whose footprints
surround our muddy tarn
that marinades giardia
from the carcass of a doe.

As God lays a lit match
to the tinderbox of old growth,
Jack glows sinisterly above
Hell's basin. A fierce star rises.

Single Litre Engine

And suddenly you're behind the wheel in something someone's
dad would drive, no spoilers or go faster stripes, or music
playing loudly to impress the girls at traffic lights,

but a vehicle neatly middle-aged, a body hitting sixty-five
when it should be doing seventy, because there's someone else's life
on the back seat in the Maxi-Cosi, and finally asleep.

And the you who seemed so far away, at best a speculation,
with no points on his licence, an address you've never seen inside of
and a date of birth that's history to his students,

is with you in the slip lane, checking mirrors, shifting gears,
as you merge onto the motorway, a voice inside
and in command, the man you never knew you were.

Driving home from hospital after the hottest day of the year

Something in us yearns for time alone in the night
to think upon our great and lonely stages where the stories
of our lives repeat, that frame our disappearances,
these worlds where we are not ourselves
but versions of the ones we left as,
vacantly in transit through departure lounges,
motorways and waiting rooms and terminals,
places where we watch ourselves move comfortably
in sharper suits with smaller, smarter luggage,
or indicate from petrol station forecourts in smoother
more successful cars with bodywork like silver muscle,
or slumped on a minicab's rain-slathered window,
shirking off the future having seen it all by scrolling
through the births and deaths and marriages,
or told within the tapestry of foam on a pint glass.
Your fantasy is waiting in the queue to pass security,
a canteen in the Welcome Break, beneath the platform clock,
or on the ward where now some magic doctor plies
her trade to bring back from the brink your love
who's giving birth to love. In such quarters we are held
by open time that may go on though never can –
the wheels touch down, the junction floats up into view,
and someone offstage calls your name.
Midnight arrives. The ward ejects the recent fathers
who walk the drowsy corridors while workers polish
floors to mirrors, past the night's wounded,
the road's bruised casualties in the custody of officers.
They start again their sleeping cars, their sober undertakings
waiting to be picked up by a different, less impatient man,
when home becomes the destination once again.

They may shed a tear in passing for their ancient selves
shambling from the closing pubs in pouring rain
that also staged a time-out to reflect upon its purpose
while the country bathed itself in sun, as something
soft and comforting escapes the radio
and the whole night begins to be as perfect as an advert
that knows that time can be distracted but never
ended. They keep their vehicles steady now all traffic
seems too close and all of time too long to pass alone.

There's been talk

of a child born on Cheapside
with a wolf's tail and goat's breasts,
of Quakers down Cannon Street with pans of fire on their heads,

and months ago, in June, the city suffered
an eclipse. Now it's Popish emissaries
throwing flames into the homes of Protestants.

They may ban our Merry Andrews, Jack Puddings, puppet shows,
or create the fasting days as though it pleased the Lord to see
the walking bones of children. Though men who work

neck-deep in death, who pawn the rings and talismans
robbed from those they lay to rest, still walk and breathe,
their skin unjudged. We're yet to build Jerusalem.

Sleeping on the top floor of a Travelodge while below another night begins

Sirens subjugate pedestrians whose voices are sirens themselves.
The Scala gently rocks, its brickwork quivering
from the bass drum of a rock band's only Number One.
When the Tube rattles by, the baby's arms reach

to grip onto air. What's become of the woman
soliciting in a soiled dress on Shaftesbury Avenue
with her gammy leg? Or the girl on the Embankment
sobbing into her fairy ring of glossy magazines?

And where's the man with lank hair, who dresses only in brown,
who appears in Argyle Square from the heart of a tree?
The all-night signs of food and wine blaze neon promises.
While we attend to sleep, who's putting out the fires?

Shade

and when she needed feeding we fed her
in graveyards on benches covered with lichen
beneath palms and succulents
with a damp flannel we cooled her head
by the Metcalfes and Tregarthens
who tired of tears and the damning of drivers
by the living Metcalfes and Tregarthens
stood cooing at the sight of our girl
in a language we know as the breeze
and when she needed feeding again
we sat by the stone in the shade of the abbey
all the while our baby was sucking
your breast that filled up like a cistern
the minute she stopped the dead leaned in
with their odour of milk pursing their lips
as though to kiss our baby's head
in the growing shade they bring with them

Night Change

I step across the moon,
the small hand

of the clock,
to lay the bundle

of my daughter down,
knowing where

the flooring waits
to exhale.

Night remembers
other nights.

I alight from one life
into another,

from my long
and sobering walk

and creak down
to my knees,

a father, still a child
bowing

to repay his debt.

Hail!

who've ranked at all points of your life from Moorfields
to Great Ormond Street, UCL, Imperial, to old
and modern pastimes – musicals, Soho revues, the BBC
on Aldwych, Wembley, the Royal Courts of Justice;

who know the year by changes in technology,
slang, fashion, politics, who've worked for you the tourist,
employee, student, wedding guest, and listened to your milestones,
grievances and ill-informed opinions on the state;

who've risked muggings for their floats, black eyes
from the drunks, the cons of bilkers, runners, jokers,
and wiped the seats clean after couples who paid for laps
around the park have tipped twice the fare and left;

who've taken us to pay respects to St Paul's
and Monument, Whitehall, the Cenotaph, and ferried us
across the bridges down from Westminster to Lambeth,
as the wheel on Southbank detonates with fireworks;

who are the ground troops of the city, supplying
commerce with resources, who are mobile confession booths,
spreading gossip like dioxide, who know the outcomes
of elections before the elected; who aren't the unlicensed

who solicit by kebab shops (their insurance underwritten
by free market politics), and have you feeling every pothole,
the history unburied in the knots of your spine,
as they swerve to miss the doors death leaves ajar;

but who are older than democracy, whom Cromwell
chartered at the time of his ill-starred republic, who pre-date
the Civil War, Samuel Pepys and Johnson, the baker's fire,
Napoleon, Jack the Ripper, Churchill.

I hail you scholars of the road, hoodless steersmen
driving hansom hackney carriages. You are the city's sleek
and shuttling spirit. Long may you rule these streets
and your takings rise beyond the plutocracy of minicabs.

May you be there at the end to drive my family
and friends home from the inevitable, and be there ranked
when it's their time, to ferry them as they awake
to find their tongues are burning with the boatman's fare.

The clear and present day

Please, in the morning when I'm vulnerable and caring,
when the sun's still gentle to its audience of grass,
when I've only started breathing, please refresh the end,
what we thought was coming, what we've learned to expect
like an encore at the concert, applause rising quickly,
timed like a sitcom's laughter at the ordinary jokes;

remind me where it started, how, before the credits rolled
their perfect lives were tangled, their marriages in tatters,
their reputations sullied, tell me, what inciting incident
sparked the flight or crossing, what underlined the tension,
a business in the doldrums or a parent's sudden death;
tell me how she felt and what she said as she approached by ferry,

as she opened up the shutters, pulled dust sheets
from furniture as though she was uncovering a ghost;
and tell me of the town he knew, its bankrupt schools,
demolished pubs and filled-in village green, the market
bare of fish and scales, no means to weigh his sighs;
and tell me of the moment when they first locked eyes,

what flowers both laid at the grave, and what outside
the baggage desk or terminal their last words to each other were,
before their long pause at the gate, and why I should be
thinking of this just as I am coming to, just as I'm returning
to what it is I'm breathing for, the clear and present day
rattling in the green light of the monitor, crying for rescue.

Prayer at the Edge of the West

Now everyone is sleeping with all doors
and windows locked, and lights switched off, the kids
below our room, silent, hooked to their devices,

I can at last go out into the cold, away from the radio's
weather reports and baseball scores, to where
salt-softened anchors of fir splinter across the beach,

to hear night's hollow note resound
inside the space I've cleared within myself,
where a forest is becoming sea.

Slowly, red lights of the buoys declare the oasis
of the shoreline, the far edge of the West,
to fishermen still trawling for their unmet quotas.

Somewhere between settled night
and the wingtip of morning, Pacific time is stopping
like a boat that runs on fumes,

beyond the pull of East and West, where edge
becomes centre and the centre edge,
and time alone can be itself, and bait and cast a line.

ACKNOWLEDGEMENTS

Acknowledgements and thanks are due to the editors of the following journals and anthologies where a number of these poems, or earlier versions of them, first appeared: *Ambit, And Other Poems, Avis Magazine, Butcher's Dog, Land of Three Rivers: The Poetry of North-East England* (Bloodaxe Books, 2017), *Northern Poetry Library, The North, Poetry Ireland Review, Poetry London, Poetry Salzburg Review, The PoetTrio Experiment, The Pushcart Prize XL: Best of the Small Presses* (W.W. Norton & Company, 2016), *The Rialto, Stand, Staying Human: new poems for Staying Alive* (Bloodaxe Books, 2020), *Steps in Time* (NCLA), *Waves and Bones* (NCLA), *Wild Court*, and *Under the Radar*.

'To a Coal-fired Power Station' was commissioned as part of a residency at the Northern Poetry Library in 2015/16 and was featured in an exhibition at Woodhorn Museum. 'There may be thawing damage' was written for *The PoetTrio Experiment* and gathers and transforms language from Robert Ettinger's *The Prospect of Immortality*, Jo Shapcott's 'Electroplating the Baby', and an essay by Dr Mark Byers about Shapcott's poem. 'Advertising' was awarded a Pushcart Prize in 2015 by Kim Addonizio and David Bottoms. 'The Knowledge' and 'Hansard' were broadcast on BBC Radio 4 on *The Echo Chamber* in 2014.

Many thanks to Wolfgang Görtschacher for publishing my pamphlet, *The Black Cab* (Poetry Salzburg, 2017), where some of these poems first appeared. I am grateful to The Poetry Trust for an Aldeburgh Eight bursary in 2015; to New Writing North for their continuing support and for selecting *The Black Cab* as a 2019 Read Regional title; and to the School of English Literature, Language and Linguistics at Newcastle University whose Research Support Fund provided time to work on this collection.

I am indebted to Sean O'Brien for his tireless support and guidance; to Neil Astley and everyone at Bloodaxe Books; to Linda Anderson, Daniel Hardisty, Wendy Heath, Keith Hutson, Jake Morris-Campbell, Sinéad Morrissey, David Spittle, Gerry Wardle, and the members of the Northern Poetry Workshop: the enthusiasm and generosity from you all has been vital. My final gratitude is reserved for Kris Johnson, whose unwavering personal and professional support has made finishing this book possible.